GINNYMARIE M. LEINES & RUTH M. GODFREY

THE
JOURNAL

MANDALA
AND THE
BUTTERFLY

The Journal
MANDALA AND THE BUTTERFLY

iUniverse books may be ordered through booksellers or by contacting:

iUniverse
1663 Liberty Drive
Bloomington, IN 47403
www.iuniverse.com
844-349-9409

IISBN: 978-1-5320-9977-9 (sc)
ISBN: 978-1-5320-9978-6 (e)

Library of Congress Control Number: 2021904270

Print information available on the last page.

iUniverse rev. date: 04/24/2021

THE
JOURNAL

MANDALA
AND THE
BUTTERFLY

Artist & Illustrator Ginnymarie M. Leines

Letter to Our Dreamers

We invite you to celebrate your dreams with *THE JOURNAL Mandala and The Butterfly.* Your inner knowing leads you to self-discovery on a new path. You are the world's 2 percent who is moving toward the manifestation of your dreams. You will land in unknown places, becoming your dreams and the visions they have given you.

Have fun, laugh often, and love yourself.

We applaud and admire you.

Ginnymarie and Ruthie

A dream landed on me today
And whispered in my ear.

Wake up! Wake up!
The world is tired of sleeping.

A dream landed on me today.
And caused my heart to leap.

Jump high! Jump high?
There is something just within your reach.

A dream landed on me today
And caused my nose to itch.

Listen up? Listen up!
The world is about to reveal its secrets.

A dream landed on me today
And begged my feet to dance.

Stomp your feet! Clap your hands! Twirl around!
The world is giving you a beat.

A dream landed on me today.

Ruth M. Godfrey

Contents

Dear Creative Soul,
We invite you to dance in celebration
As you breathe life into your dreams.
Ginnymarie and Ruthie

Mandala and the Butterfly Actions

You will experience how it is to be still, be discerning, be trusting, and be your dreams through the *Mandala and the Butterfly, The Journal*

Be Still

Our lives are filled with noise, static, and disruption. Being still calls us to the present moment of silence. It is in the silence we discover who we are being called to be.

Be Discerning

Our world is continually moving, shifting, and changing. We are challenged to separate facts from story, finding messages designed for our unique selves.

Be Trusting

We can find a way to trust who we are called to be by pushing through all internal and external resistance.

Be Your Dreams

When we step into a bigger story of how we see ourselves, our dreams become far-reaching and can flourish beyond imagination.

Chapter 1
Be Still

Create time and space to reflect.

Quiet your mind; simply be.

Slow down and unplug.

It will bring clarity of purpose.

Belief

When you are still, you can observe your internal thoughts and feelings.

The best way to be in tune to your dreams is to first be still. Being still invites you to listen. When you quiet your mind and listen, you sharpen your ability to learn, to focus, to concentrate, and to be open to possibilities.

In stillness, you will recognize your thoughts and feelings. Your dream paths start with how you choose to create your subconscious. Each of us has negative thoughts. You have the power to allow them to be fleeting thoughts.

How you respond is how you interact with yourself, others, and the world around you.

Great questions to ask:

What will it take for you to be still?

What might get in your way?

How can you release negative thoughts and feelings?

I have learned to Be Still & Listen.

I listen to My Thoughts …

My feelings.

I listen to My Heart.

It is Difficult to know Who is Speaking.

Is it My thoughts, My feelings, My heart, My ego …

I am learning to Distinguish

Between these Voices.

—Christina Arnold

Belief

When you are still, you can discover what is truly important.

Your dreams will take on greater meaning when you uncover what their message is. Embrace your dreams, find them, own them, and make them who you are.

Become your dreams. Feel them take flight.

Great questions to ask:

What are your dreams?

What riddles are your dreams revealing about who you are?

How can you solve your riddles?

When I am Still

Trust begins to emerge.

When it fully arrives,

my inner knowing reminds me to

"Place my future into God's hands."

When I do—

I Feel Confident.

I am Brave.

—Scott Kearns

Belief

When you are still, you find your sense of place in the world.

Stillness helps you sink more deeply into where you are at the moment. When you are still, you can discover who you are. Stillness renews your sense of self in the world by grounding you. It allows you to feel the richness of your connectivity.

Your dreams will find you.

Great questions to ask:

How will your dreams give you a place to stand in the world?

What will you have to do differently?

What questions are your dreams begging you to answer?

Your Dream Will Find You

It is what It is.

You Can Hide From It

You Can Hold Hands With It

You Can Cover It Up With A Blanket

And It Will Still Find You.

—Heidi Tuneberg

Actions for You: Be Still

Wake up.

Find a place to sit by a window.

Just be.

Observe.

What do you notice?

Chapter 2
Be Discerning

Our world is continually moving, shifting, and changing. We are challenged to separate facts from story, finding messages designed for our unique selves.

Be discerning. Find what parts of your dreams are yours to breathe life into. When you are discerning, you make decisions that honor you. You can realize what gives you life.

Belief

Discernment depends on your powerful questions. Asking powerful questions takes practice. It requires thoughtfulness. Powerful questions lead you to solid answers. They are a dynamic tool in uncovering next steps. When asking a question, think about what you want the question to do or provide.

Great questions to ask:

What is your gut feeling about the dreams that have a grip on you?

What tells you these dreams are for you?

How can you allow your heart and head to work together to fulfill your dreams?

Discernment begins with the BIGGEST & BEST QUESTIONS.

What puzzle pieces are holding me back?

Who will help me find my missing pieces?

How can I know that I Have the BIGGEST & BEST ANSWERS?

—Tanner Antolak

Belief

Discernment serves as our catalyst to action. We want to take the best actions. Many people stall because they aren't certain how their dreams will evolve. They want to know how things will turn out before they get started. The reality is when we start breathing life into our dreams, we may experience an obscure pathway clouded with heavy fog. Embracing fog and stepping through it will cause it to dissipate.

Minimize distractions knowing your discernment is carrying you.

Great questions to ask:

What is carrying you through the fog?

What scares you about what's on the other side?

What are you most excited about?

It's the right time to take flight

when the feeling is with me during the day & visits me at night.

It tells me it entered my soul & won't release me

Until I make something happen.

—Jennie Antolak

Belief

Discernment calls us to our truth. Our truth lies in how we perceive ourselves and what we believe our roles are in living our dreams. Our truth cannot be discerned by others. Our responsiveness to our dreams is often limited by our beliefs. This can result in resistance. We resist what we may believe our dreams will ask of us. We resist our dreams when we believe we have to conform to those around us. We resist when our internal desire to fit in is stronger than our belief in our dreams. We sometimes think it is easier to stay in our comfort zone. We often settle, conforming and distancing ourselves from our dreams.

Great questions to ask:

How is your self-image reflected in your dreams?

What assumptions and biases do you have about who you are in the world?

What pull do people have that distracts you from your truth?

When I work from my Heart,

The Good, the Exact, The Perfect Place calls Me to Walk my Path,

Allowing Source to Manifest My Life instead of Me.

—Dave Powers

Actions for You: Be Discerning

Imagine four key words which describe parts of your dreams.

Draw a mandala circle. Divide it into eight parts. Use a different colored marker for each section. Write each word in a section of the mandala.

How do your words create action?

What small action will set you on your path?

Chapter 3
Be Trusting

We can find a way to trust who we are called to be by pushing through internal and external resistance.

Be trusting. Believe your dreams are yours to live.

To be trusting calls you to listen to intuitions, symbols, and signs.

They give you clues how to breathe life into your dreams.

Belief

Trust creates hope, giving us the promise we can live our dreams. We lean into hope when we trust. We experience throughout our life journey how trust has served us in the past.

Trust calls on faith.

Faith calls on belief.

Belief calls on imagination.

Imagination calls on dreams.

—Ginnymarie and Ruthie

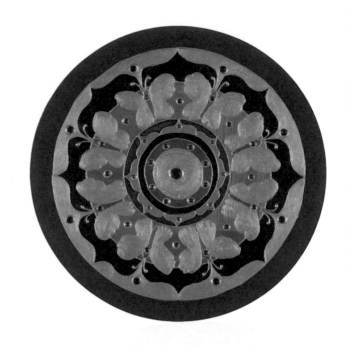

Great questions to ask:

What will it take for you to trust your signs and messages?

What will it feel like to trust?

How will trust move you closer to manifesting your dreams?

Belief

When you trust, your intuition surfaces. Trust creates feelings rooted in self-discovery and realization. It invites you to recognize your ability to take action. When you do, you have given yourself permission to step into your dreams.

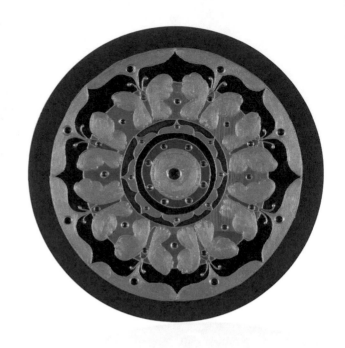

Great questions to ask:

What intuitions have you trusted?

What actions did they prompt you to take?

What intuitions are surfacing today?

Work hard

Trust all is Well.

Believe in Possibility

Your Destination will find you.

Life Is The Art of The Possible.

—Dr. Kenneth Libre

Belief

The importance of trusting is alive in you. Trust gives you the joy of hope. Hope diminishes fear, doubt, and anxiety. Hope provides open channels to listening, seeing, and feeling. Your intuition signals you to step into your dreams. It gives you the power to believe what you know can be and is true for you.

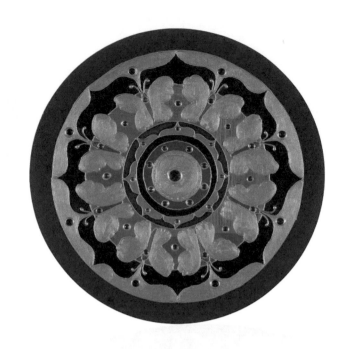

Great questions to ask:

Where does trust show up in your daily life?

When has trust diminished fear, doubt, and anxiety?

How have your feelings created hope for you?

Fear,

I know how to deal with you.

There is no going under,
Over or around

Only through you.

I now know descending into your belly.
I have the power to pull the curtains back.

When I do,
I am surprised
A flood of light appears.
It washes a new color over me.

I am no longer frightened
By you.

I can move in and out
Of your intense spaces.

Vulnerable to every wisp of air,
I sit, I trust, I hold space,
eventually I emerge.

—Dr. Zoë Robbins

Actions for You: Be Trusting

Download pictures of your dream journeys.

Imagine the places in the world your dreams will take you.

Capture those moments before they happen with your dream flight board.

Observe: feel the excitement and energy as your dreams become your reality.

Chapter 4
Be Your Dreams

When you step into a bigger story of how you see yourself, your dreams become far-reaching. They will flourish in ways you never imagined.

Be your dreams. Allow your dreams to flourish.

To become your dreams, breathe life into them.

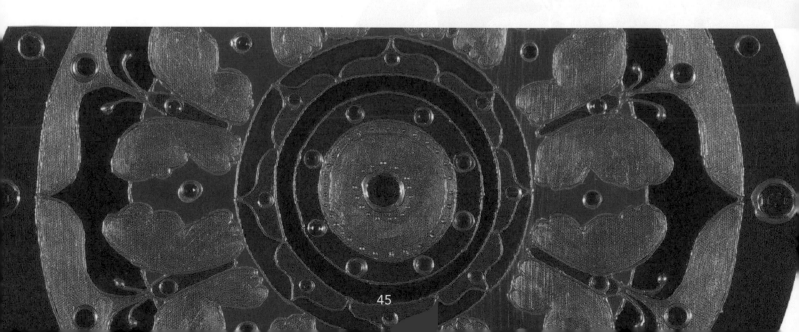

Belief

The highest level of being is to become your dreams and to flourish with them. This creates a ripple effect that the world can feel, benefit from, and celebrate with you. It effects the people we know and love. When you are open to becoming your dreams, you have given yourself permission to live and be your truth.

Great questions to ask:

What are you feeling today as you become your dreams?

What do you imagine will change for the people around you?

How can you give yourself permission to take flight with your dreams?

When Pursuing a Dream,

Hold Steadfast

To Your willingness To Fail.

—Carol Ann Docken Fisher

Belief

When you become your dreams, the world awakens around you, filled with surprises. Your life has new messages and signs. You can control how you respond; however, you cannot control people's reactions. You are being put on notice to stay clear of distractions.

Great questions to ask:

How has the awakened world impacted your dreams?

What has puzzled you?

What new signs and messages are signaling next steps?

It Doesn't Happen Overnight,

You Must Work Like Crazy,

I'm Living Proof That It's Completely Possible

To Build Something Out of Nothing.

—Kristen Bor

Belief

When you become your dreams, you realize your gifts. The true essence of life is to reach your highest self. Your purpose on earth is to become your dreams.

Great questions to ask:

How are you recognizing the value of your dreams?

What are you mindful of as you are becoming your dreams?

How will becoming your dreams inspire others?

Actions For You

Become your dreams.

Host a dream-flight party.

Invite your tribe, the people who stand with you.

It is time for you to show and tell.

Celebrate your dreams.

Acknowledgments

We are fascinated by and grateful for the inspirational messages shared by our contributors. We thank our many friends who have inspired us through our greater vision of possibility for humankind. A special thank-you to Jennie Antolak, Aunt Franny, Barbie Ingram,Doug Blake,Darci Watson, Tracy Off,Paul Heusssenstamm,our cherished families, friends, and the students and graduates of The International Center of Coaching, Learning Journeys.

What the caterpillar calls the end, The rest of the world calls a butterfly
Lao Tzu

About the Authors

Ruth Godfrey is the founder of the International Center of Coaching, Learning Journeys, which she co-owns with her daughter, Jennie Antolak. Exploring the ideas of <u>Mandala and The Butterfly</u> has been a creative structural placeholder for her. The writing experience continually reminded her of the importance of breathing life into dreams. She lives in Woodbury, Minnesota. She has three adult children and five precocious grandchildren. Her wish for all readers is to become the soul of their journeys, allowing their dreams to take flight. The following are some of her professional credentials: Master of Science, Adult and Occupational Education, Kansas State University, Bachelor of Science, Recreational Leadership, University of Minnesota, master certified coach, designated by the International Coach Federation; certified narrative coach practitioner. She is the co-author of *Delicious Conversations and Coach on the Run 10: A Way of Being.*

www.learningjourneys.net

Curious, inquisitive, and a seeker of the mysteries and adventures of life, Ginnymarie M. Leines is a master certified coach and narrative coach practitioner from the International Center of Coaching, Learning Journeys. She loves people, listening to their stories, and delighting in their vision and possibility. A businesswoman, entrepreneur, international manufacturer, designer, artist, and educator; she is the mother of three sons and three daughters (in-law), grandmother to eight grandchildren, and lover of Gregory, her husband and partner of fifty years. She lives at Alta, Utah. The following are some of her professional credentials: Bachelor of Science, Language Arts, English, Secondary Education, Journalism, and Communciation, Hamline University, St. Paul, Minnesota. University of Minnesota, Leadership Training Certification, Seven Habits of Highly Effective People.

www.ginnymarieleines.com

Printed in the United States
by Baker & Taylor Publisher Services